Developing a Champion
SPIRIT
In just 10 minutes

For Women Only

Mikel Brown

Developing a Champion
SPIRIT
In just 10 minutes

For Women Only

Mikel Brown

PUBLISHING COMPANY

EL PASO, TEXAS

Developing the Champion Spirit in just 10 minutes

For Women Only

C
CJ PUBLISHING
C   COMPANY

1208 Sumac Drive
El Paso, TX 79925

Copyright © 2005 by Mikel Brown
Printed in the United States of America
Library of Congress Control Number:
ISBN: 1-930388-12-8

Editorial assistance for CJC Publishing Co. by Gary Sparkman

All scriptures are taken from the King James Version and the New International Version

Cover design by C.Hughes Advertising Agency

Published by CJC Publishing Company

All rights reserved. No portion of this book may be used without the written permission of the publisher, with the exception of brief excerpts in magazine articles, reviews, etc. For further information or permission, address CJC Publishing Co. 1208 Sumac Drive, El Paso, Texas 79925

Table of Contents

DEDICATION..V

SPECIAL THANKS...VI

PREFACE...VII

CHAPTER 1
Developing the Champion in You.......................................2

CHAPTER 2
Women Overcoming Self-Doubt.......................................22

CHAPTER 3
His Money is Your Business..34

CHAPTER 4
Understanding The Principle of Money...........................40

CHAPTER 5
The New Power Woman..46

CHAPTER 6
Secrets to Personal Success...54

MEDALLIONS OF HONOR..59

NOTES..60

ABOUT THE AUTHOR...62

IV

Dedication

To my lifelong friend and wife for her unselfish devotion to me and my calling. To my children Joshua, Mikayla, Mikelle, Marquita, and Mikel Jr. who are part of the generation to which I've dedicated my efforts: to the many people whose lives will be touched and forever changed after reading this book.

Special Thanks

My heartfelt thanks and deepest appreciation to the following spiritual sons and daughters, and friends whose financial seeds have enabled the consummation of this project. I Love You!

Savaslas & Tracey Lofton (Music in my ear)
Derrick & Varonica Jones
Alan & Alma Spence
Reggie & Nancy Mainor
Scott & Laura Whittle
Roy & Tish Times
Gregory & Monica Austin
Bryan & Tracie Reed
Jameelah Joshua
Willie & Katherine Jenkins
Bill & Becky Smith

Preface

Dr. Mikel Brown usually starts his lectures by saying, "Hi, I'm Mikel Brown and it's good to be a winner!" Winning in life doesn't always equate to winning a contest. A contest of sports or game is not as important as life itself. One thing is for certain; no one really enjoys losing. And when life seems to be going in a downward spiral, you need to quickly figure out how to get your life back on the up swing. It might seem incredible that you can turn your situation around, but everywhere people are raving about Dr. Mikel Brown's amazing tips on how to develop a winning edge. "***Developing a Champion Spirit: In just Ten Minutes***" will give you the tools and tactical approach on how YOU can be a Winner in Life.

VIII

Chapter 1

Developing the Champion in You

Chapter 1

Developing the Champion in You

It doesn't take long to develop a Champion's Spirit; it simply takes patience to allow the process to unfold. Integrity, Character, Strength, and Leadership are four qualities that define a Champion. Personally, I'd rather be in control rather than under the control of someone else. Accepting the condition of being under control may suggest a mindset toward passivity. However, the desire to control your own destiny would tend to imply an inward proclivity toward an assertive disposition. People will basically subscribe to one of two worldviews regarding their lot in life. The first view places them in complete control of their environment, while individuals in the other category see themselves as the ruled, with little control over their existence. There is a vast difference between the two viewpoints.

Your struggles in life must be viewed as assignments, designed to expose your weaknesses so that you can expel them from your life. The struggles surface to prepare you for subsequent tests along the path of your destiny. You should never take life's tests without first studying your assignment. We have all, at some point in our lives, held secret fears of not being able to live up to the images we have projected to others. People are always looking for admiration and respect from others. The problem is that while we are learning how to be individuals of courage and integrity, we must do so in a world full of compromise. Champions are not those who never fail; they are those who never quit. Men and women who have never failed are usually those who have never set their minds to do anything. The difference between people who succeed and those who fail lie in their ability to handle the pressures that mount against them.

Character is defined by more than just talent and ability. Everyone has talent, but not everyone has character. Each of us must summons the courage to rely upon the integrity that resides deep within the heart of all of us. Everyone has his or her own core character values, and no one can duplicate anyone else's. The appeal of strong character serves to attract those searching for a fixed standard of excellence.

Within each of us lie amazing qualities that are not easily discerned. However, you must be tenacious enough to dig beneath the debris of failure, hurt and discouragement to find your hidden treasure. You must not tire in your quest to discover it. Perseverance will greatly assist you in your pursuits.

The bully whom you must face in life today as an adult is not necessarily the big, bad neighbor down the street. At this stage, the bully comes in the form of procrastination, bad habits, intimidation, negativity, unfortunate past childhood experiences, and cowardice; they are all designed to test your resolve to win in life.

Your life will not improve simply because you hope for it. It will only get better after you take the necessary steps to bring about the type of change you desire. If you do not exercise and eat right, your body will not function optimally. The same principle holds true in life. In order to make life work for you, you must apply certain principles and be willing to learn. It doesn't take long to develop a Champion's Spirit; it simply takes patience to allow the process to unfold.

C is for Courage

Valor doesn't mean that you are invincible, it just indicates that you have the audacity to stand in the face of the opposition and declare your position.

We live in a world where attempts at success are rewarded the same as the actual achievement. In actuality, no frail attempts at victory have ever produced winning results. Each year thousands of men and women join our armed forces and swear an oath to defend our constitution. However, when the time comes to actually fulfill their oaths, some then choose to conveniently declare conscientious objector status. The amazing part is that they never object to receiving any of the benefits that go along with wearing the uniform. Yet these same military personnel would stand in line for hours to receive a Purple Heart - - - for a yellow back.

A Champion must have the fortitude to follow through with commitment. Courage is always tested, or how else can we recognize its authenticity. The mistaken belief is that brave individuals face their opposition because they lack fear. The contrary is true. By overcoming their fears to face their opponents, individuals are then recognized as brave. To become brave, you must, at some point in your life, realize that it is better to fight on your feet than to serve on your knees.

Power words for Courage: bravery, courageousness, daring, dauntlessness, doughtiness, fearlessness, gallantry, guts, hardihood, heart, heroism, intrepidity, intrepidness, nerve, stoutness, valor, backbone, fortitude, grit, gumption, spunk, determination, perseverance, resolution, endurance, stamina, tenacity, audacity, boldness, brazenness, cheek, gall, temerity.

H is for Honor

Honor is the high estimation of a person who has gained the respect, consideration and veneration for doing what comes normal for them.

That which rightfully attracts esteem, respect, or consideration is not what you do, but how you do it! Athletes learn early on how to employ dirty tactics to gain the advantage against their opponents. However, if they are guided by an inward standard of self-respect, they will learn to accept winning or losing according to set rules.

Self-respect is better than people's respect. If you honor yourself, you will command respect from others without ever saying a word. When I look at people, I focus not only on physical appearances, but also on how people comport themselves. The person with nothing to prove is not overly concerned with what others think of him or her. This person refuses to live according to expectations of others.

A title is not honor, it's a label. Honor is an ornament of excellence and distinction. People of honor will put in the hours necessary to make their lives, marriages, businesses, churches, and relationships work. They know that it is not what you do that earns people's respect; it's simply how you do it.

Power words for Honor: dignity, courage, fidelity, especially, excellence of character, high moral worth, virtue, nobleness, integrity, uprightness, trustworthiness, in women, purity, chastity.

A is for Authority

When you recognize your power or authority, you must also identify the scope of it as well.

You have an ordained right to govern your life and live it as you choose. It is unfortunate, however, when people look to others to captain their lives. You are in your own custody, and you have the power to make all decisions concerning your life.

Power is weakness in the hands of the one who does not recognize its potential. Each person is in position to make his or her world into what is desired. However, millions of people would consciously leave their lives in the hands of fate. "Whatever will be, will be!" is their motto. This should not be the mantra that governs your life. It should actually be "Whatever you want to be, will be!"

You have the right to command how you want your life to turn out. Champions understand, by virtue of their status as humans, that they own the right to determine their course in life. As long as your brain is working, and your body is functional, people must learn to pilot their own lives. You can make your world as small or as large as you would like for it to be. That decision-making authority rests within each of us.

Power is simply authority, and authority must have its jurisdiction. Parents have jurisdiction over the life of their children. From this, we cannot conclude that the two people who are biologically responsible for producing a child are also the parents of that child. Parenthood implies so much more. In essence, the parents are the ones who feed, nurture, clothe, and educate their children. Dead beat mothers and dads are not parents in the true sense of the word. A true champion understands the areas where improvement is needed, even if improvement means facing embarrassing and humiliating circumstances for the purpose of teaching their children the importance of taking responsibility for one's actions.

People are not relegated to failure for the rest of their lives because they may have made some bad decisions. Get up from your despondent position and use your authority to turn your life around. Speak to your situation and command it to dissolve and dry up from the roots.

Power words for Authority: Legal, power, command, ability, strength, clout, influence, right, compel, force, and energy.

M is for Maturity

When a person can live with his or her past without being bogged down by it, he or she remains adaptable and capable to continue the process of change for a better life.

If an individual is going to grow toward the type of maturity that will foster a healthy self-esteem, it can only be built on a solid and unyielding foundation. Two major characteristics of maturity are the presence of wisdom and knowledge. They will help the person to be at home with realities, and not slide into a fantasy world of the make believe.

A child sees a puddle of water and jumps right into the middle of it, spattering water every where. A mature minded person sees the puddle of water and walks around it. This may sound simple to you now, but I assure you that when you were a young kid, the puddle of water was very tempting.

How a person handles responsibility reveals the level of their maturity. Taking responsibility for one's actions is a strong predictor of whether one will succeed in business and in life. Mature individuals can be ribald or genteel, sweet or acid, cheerful or gloomy, but the important point is that they be alive, with vigorous interests that make them interesting to be with. They should have a sense of humor because it helps to dilute the frustrations that one may encounter.

The mature person knows that he has to go on making decisions that are of little importance and of great importance; and that each option will cost him something. He knows that his integrity is continually susceptible to practical demands, seductive temptations, concessions, compromises and conflicting values, but that it can only be preserved at the cost of some spiritual and mental energy being exerted.

Power words for Maturity: Realistic, decisive, responsible, developed, accountable, dependable, sensible, level-hearted, conscientious, and constant.

P is for Principles

The level of your present quality of life is all based on the principles you choose to be governed by.

The choices people make are influenced by their individual belief system. Principles are nothing more than a governing system of beliefs established by an individual that determines life's choices. Every principle is not necessarily a good principle. Principles govern all of our actions—even if the action is good, bad, or indifferent. When people say that they have morals, they are actually saying that they live by principles.

The principle of success is revealed in the mechanics of it. If a person desires to be successful, they must learn how success works. Success does not happen inadvertently as though one succeeds in spite of being ignorant. It is a deliberate attempt to follow through on the rules of engagement concerning success. If success is a game, then there must be rules or laws that dictate how it is played...rules that will guarantee your success every time.

"I hated every minute of training, but I said,

> 'Don't quit. Suffer now and live the rest of your life as a champion." —Muhammad Ali

Aristotle said "Excellence is not an act, but a habit." I am a firm believer that success is not an accident. Unlike millions of Americans, who play the lottery in hopes that they will one day buy the winning ticket, I believe that I am the winning ticket. My future will rise or fall on my willingness to submit to the regimen of preparation that will lead me to success. Every winner in life has one common trait; they have learned to master the fundamentals or principles.

A boxer who is vigorous in his training realizes that victory comes in the training, and not in the actual fight. Your willingness to prepare and to be coached or mentored is evidence of your passion and desire to succeed. You cannot escape this fundamental principle of success. If a person's marriage fails or if a business does not succeed, you better believe that those failures can be traced back to either refusing to listen to sound counsel or refusing to adhere to the principles that are necessary to finish what was started.

A champion has all the traits of a winner. They have qualified and employed the services of a key person (life coach) who has a proven track record of providing sound, results-producing counsel regarding matters of interest. The qualified mentor or life coach must have an established belief system based on truth and not fantasy. It should be evident that they have engaged their mental faculty for both the development of their body and sound habits. They are people of principles and not preference. Preferences are negotiable, but principles are non-negotiable.

Power words for Principles: truth, basics, essentials, fundamentals, rudiments, foundation, groundwork, nitty-gritty, belief, canon, doctrine, dogma, faith, philosophy, axiom, law, precept, tenet, rule, and standard.

I is for Integrity

The integrity of a person is not just in their ability to speak the truth, but also in their power to live it.

Integrity seems to be a dying art in society. The quality or the state of being complete is integrity in force. Soundness and sobriety are qualities that are tantamount to integrity and should be viewed as an essential component to a person's success.

In times of antiquity, the Roman soldiers (innovators of the two-edged sword) would properly manufacture and test the quality of their sword before sending their soldiers into battle with them. The process was unique because the producer of this kind of weaponry had to ensure and vouch with their life that these swords would not break under pressure. These innovative people would heat the steel until it was red hot in order that the heat would scatter the molecules so that it would be easier to beat the lack of integrity out of it. Then they would beat the steel into the shape of the sword. After the cooling process would occur, the sword constructor would again heat the sword until it was extremely hot and adaptable. The red-hot sword would expose the imperfections in the metal. These vulnerabilities had to be beaten out of the sword and then placed again in cold water in order to quickly move the molecules closer together, creating a dense metal. The process would be repeated until all the imperfections and vulnerable areas had been eliminated.

Beating the sword when it was red hot tested the integrity of it before it was taken into battle. A trained Roman soldier needed the assurance that in battle his sword would not break under the constant pounding because his life depended on it.

Champions of life have submitted themselves to the creative process of perfection. They are not interested in going into life's battle without first being battle tested. These champions in life have endured the constant pounding of a disciplined, regimented training and have been qualified and declared duly ready to overcome the challenges in their lives. In an actual battle, it is too late to test what should have been tested and examined in training. Honesty and durability describe what integrity is, but maintaining and overcoming illustrates what integrity does.

Power words for Integrity: Honesty, completeness, purity, stability, incorruption, straightforwardness, soundness, absoluteness, and forthrightness.

O is for Optimism

Optimism without faith is like a frame without a picture.

We live in a society where most people are symmetrically opposed to positive people. A person who is optimistic about a negative situation often aggravates those individuals who are pessimistic in nature. Negative people can give you a hundred reasons why you cannot succeed in your endeavors. They will start off with all the obvious external blemishes and then they will attack your character and heart. Skeptics always believe that they have more going for themselves than you have working for you. And despite your achievements, they will never allow themselves to see you any higher than they at their lowest point. This is one good reason why you should not waste your time trying to make a liar out of your critics. Instead, make a believer out of yourself. If there is anybody who needs to be convinced about your ability to succeed—it is you! If you are convinced about your abilities and you believe in you, why should you care about what others think? Your greatest victory will not come in your challenge with other people; it will only happen after you've conquered your own fears and insecurities.

Optimism is expectancy in its most generic form. OPTIMISM is an active, empowering, constructive attitude that creates conditions for success by focusing and acting on possibilities and opportunities. If a person desires to live effectively, he or she will have to root out all self-defeating pessimism and replace it with active enthusiasm.

True optimism is not forcing a smile in order to convince others that all is well. This will simply be a surface mask intended to camouflage your confusion and frustration. Once you fully understand and are persuaded of why negativity holds you back, you will be able to live practical and productive lives for the better.

Christians, pastors, businessmen, athletes, dancers, recording artists, actors and actresses, etc. are all vulnerable to the attacks of pessimism. Your greatest vulnerability to the attacks of jealousy and negativity will always stem from the success of someone in your own field of expertise. A person is seldom envious of someone in another field.

Christians should be the most positive people on the planet. Over time, some of us have only proven to be among the most negative in society. But in all actuality Christians have an active living faith residing inside of them that reveals the truth that nothing is impossible to them that believe. What a living legacy.

Champions of life are people who rise to the occasion when a negative situation arises. They have forecasted the outcome because they've calculated the win. It is important to realize life is like a battery—it needs both positive and negative connections in order to tap into its benefits and rewards.

Power words for Optimism: Anticipation, possible, happiness, idealism, positivism, resilience, cheerfulness, and enthusiasm.

N is for Notable

People of notable character are those who have done the insignificant, overlooked things for people less fortunate than themselves, which distinguishes them from the rich and famous.

Mother Teresa spent her entire life touching the lives of people who could not in turn reward her with anything but a smile and a thank you. Martin Luther King, Jr. lost his life fighting for equality for all African Americans and under privileged people in America, in spite of their race, creed, or color. Jesus did not spend the bulk of His time in ministry raising funds to support His missionary efforts. His ministry was supported and funded by those who were delivered of demons, healed of sicknesses and diseases and forgiven of their sins. He reached out to touch the forgotten and told them that God knew them by name; He preached the good news to the poor and exposed them to how to prosper; Jesus also motivated change in women that laid on their backs for a living and showed them a better way to make a living and feel good about themselves. And at the end of His human life on earth and in taking His last breath, He exclaimed, "Forgive them for they know not what they do."

Which act deserves the most distinguished reward, the work of Jesus Christ or the singing career and antics of Elvis Presley? In truth, no other act should be mentioned in the same breath with Jesus. People are noteworthy for the noble things they have done in the lives of people, not for the things they have done in order to boost their careers.

Our society is so shallow that it reveals its ugly head in most people who are only interested in becoming rich and famous. Television presents the wrong message to our kids, leaving them with few options but many inconsistencies. Moreover, adults are inundated with images of extra-marital affairs, killings, anger management problems, integrity issues in our White House, and white collar crimes where only 1 out of every 100 persons found guilty spends time in prison.

People do not generally desire to live a life of principle. They want money and fame even at the cost of their honor. Being rich and/or famous does not improve your character, nor does it eliminate your shortcomings. In these modern times, some people can become famous by acting a complete fool.

Champions of life are not shallow people looking for someone to acknowledge their noble deeds. In fact, they do not post them on the front page of the newspaper trying to get the attention of the public. A person may only hear what a Champion is doing in the lives others, from those who are direct or indirect recipients of their labor of love. Champions stand for a cause; they are not rebels without a cause.

Find a hurting person and meet their need. You don't have to look far to find a lonely person. Mark the life of the lonely with your companionship. Become interested in other people's lives and watch how they will celebrate your presence.

Power words for Notable: Worthy, remarkable, prominent, distinguished, noteworthy, memorable, nameable, renowned, and illustrious.

Chapter 2

Women Overcoming Self-Doubt

Chapter 2

Women Overcoming Self-Doubt

The power of the woman is concealed in her ability to hide her pain. I have seen women endure some of the most horrific experiences overcome the pain and the scars of a rape, and placed at the bottom of the pay scale while doing the same task and sometimes more work than her male counterparts. Yet she survives!

> *The power of the woman is concealed in her ability to hide her pain.*

History exposes us to the undeniable touch of a mother, the wisdom of a wife, and the woman's uncanny ability to run a household as well as a business. She learned to master doing more than one thing at a time. Domestically, she successfully juggles children, homework, preparing dinner while dealing with cramps and a headache all at the same time. In many cases, she works a nine to five and then comes home and continues her day to day operation.

I admire the women who are mothers and business owners at the same time. My hat goes off to their drive and perseverance against the many apparent challenges. Women are great managers because they've learned and practiced their skills in the home. Where else can you gain that kind of on-the-job training? The dynamics of a woman's leadership works best in innovative ways. Her strength for business is seen in her ability to simplify situations to make them work efficiently. I am in no way minimizing the position of the man. Nor am I pushing a matriarchal society. I am simply embracing the strengths and wisdom of the woman whom God designed to help the man.

Canadian women have been launching businesses at twice the rate of men in recent years. With the growth of Canadian exports over the last decade, there are many untapped opportunities for women in world trade. Women in America are competing at such a high level for major roles in large corporations that men are showing their insecurity colors at an even faster rate. The power of the man and the strength of the woman are to work in concert, not against one another. With my special focus on small business, I invite more women entrepreneurs to explore how my company, Power Communication Network, can help both American and Canadian businesses take advantage of the many opportunities worldwide.

I strongly believe that God is bringing back into the church the lost gift of praying women. Women have historically been pushed into the background of church society, and now, they are being forced into the workforce in alarming numbers. My aim is not to downplay the importance of praying men. However, from the very creation account in Genesis, I see the strong, supportive and enabling role that women have provided to men throughout the ages- often without the proper recognition due them. And their key role as mighty, prayer warriors is no exception. I can even make out the woman's strong presence in the Garden of Eden as a splendid silhouette, juxtaposed against the divinely-sculpted manifestation of the man.

Most Bible scholars would agree that, throughout the scriptures, God embeds hidden messages within the surface context of more superficial messages. And our quest must be to discover the message behind the message or the message within a message. Likewise, in the creation account of Genesis, God reveals the woman's coexistence within man, even at his being formed from the dust of the earth. There we see the beauty of Eve resident within Adam from the beginning.

You will never discover the beauty of the ocean by swimming on the surface. God is fully aware that if we hunger for his wisdom and knowledge, we will diligently seek his presence. God will reveal the message behind the message only to those who are inquisitive. Within every story Jesus told, there usually was a deeper message to be learned. Between every word God utters, there is a deeper revelation. Once you move beyond the surface, you will begin to see all the other mysteries unfold. You can call it figurative, prototypical, or metaphorical, but the truth remains; behind every mask, there is a face. And in God's word, there is thoughtful intent within every word spoken, and calculated purpose behind everything God does. Humanity reveals a similar modus operandi regarding God's desire to hide purpose within purpose. The woman, in this case, is a sterling example of how God hides purpose within a purpose.

> **Gene 1:26 (KJS)** And God said, Let us make man in our image, after our likeness: and let them have dominion over the fish of the sea, and over the fowl of the air, and over the cattle, and over all the earth, and over every creeping thing that creepeth upon the earth.

27 So God created man in his [own] image, in the image of God created he him; male and female created he them. 28 And God blessed them, and God said unto them, Be fruitful, and multiply, and replenish the earth, and subdue it: and have dominion over the fish of the sea, and over the fowl of the air, and over every living thing that moveth upon the earth.

Can you see the contours of the silhouette being formed? Moreover, we get a glimpse of another being hidden inside the man. Inside this passage of scripture is revealed an appendix, a supplement or a sequel to the original blueprint of man. If you look closely enough you can catch a glimpse of the outline for yourself. Believe me; it's there. As you can see in verse 27, although He [God] created him, in him [man] was them [male/female]. God then blessed them, not just him.

In the Bible, we discover that there were women who followed and supported Jesus' ministry; although, this practice was contrary to the traditions of that time and geographic locale. This co-mingling of the sexes was not a common practice. The rabbis held that the law should not be taught to women, yet Jesus allowed them to follow him and to hear his teachings. Mary Magdalene (appropriately

Women Overcoming Self-Doubt

named because she was from the village of Magdala near the Sea of Galilee) was a passionate follower of Jesus' teaching and a faithful financial contributor to his ministry. Except for the spiritual deliverance she encountered at the hand of Jesus, little is known about her life beyond that experience.

Joanna is another great example of a woman who fell in love with Christ's teachings and demonstrated her appreciation for it through her giving. Joanna was the wife of Chuzâ, and he was someone who held a very prominent position within Herod's administration. Chuzâ, many scholars believe, was the same nobleman mentioned in St. John 4:46-53 who received noteworthy mention because his entire household believed. As a result of his wealth, Joanna was able to direct much of it toward supporting Jesus and his staff of disciples. Again, the bible does not reveal much about her life outside of her benevolence. Furthermore, Susanna was another biblical character whose only claim to fame is linked to her generous support of Jesus' ministry.

These women used their means to lend financial support to Jesus' evangelistic efforts. The very fact that Jesus had a staff of men following him required that he have a base of financial support to provide for their practical needs. More often than not, it was women who stepped up to the plate to finance the Gospel work. In essence, these early financiers of the evangelization of the Gospel are the first recorded indications of a woman's missionary society for the support of spreading the Gospel.

There was a woman that originally came to me after leaving an abusive relationship, a single mother of two boys, and living with her parents. She wore earrings in the most unlikely spot, her face. But that didn't deter me from reaching out to her. I saw great potential under the debris of hurt and desperation and decided to not only pray diligently for her, but to encourage her despite the many bad decisions she's made throughout her life. I saw her battling to find her identity while trying to escape from her past, only to see her fall back helplessly into the same traps brought on from having a lack of integrity. Yet, she was determined to make things right and live her dreams. At times, she took short cuts that only lead her back into the spiral downfall she just crawled out from.

I don't believe she realized the power of her potential and the tenacity to her pursuit. I could see the little steps she was making to develop her character although she would fall prey to the challenges that presented themselves to her which tested her progress in that area. Still she went forward. She was once told that she had a welfare mentality which almost crushed her world. She thought perhaps by being a single parent, people would see her making an effort and reward her for her valiant effort. We live in a world that loves heroes, successful and rich people, but we have very little sympathy for frail attempts and weak minded people. Decisions had to be made, and she came to the conclusion that it would not be by the person that made that dreadful statement to her. She may not have wanted to hear that unforgettable statement, but it caused her to work harder and set out to prove that she could do it alone. Wrong idea! That kind of attitude only leads to ruin. If you need to prove anything to anybody—you need to prove it to yourself.

I saw her listening more intently to the words I spoke in my lectures and could finally see some major improvements in the integrity area of her life. She was not quite out of the woods yet, but at least she was on her way. Suddenly, a man came into her life and loved her two boys as much as he loved her. They were married and lived... well struggled to live happily ever after. They were happy together, but they were miserable financially. Her baggage and his baggage crossed the marriage barrier and it looked like disaster would surely destroy their relationship. Others saw them

Developing A Champion Spirit – in just 10 minutes

make one bad decision after another and many washed their hands of them. I personally don't believe in following the crowd, so the crowd went on without my approval and sentenced them to failure. Still I believed in her intrinsic ability to plow ahead, especially if she was told that she could. It is great to believe in yourself but it is far greater when someone else believes in you.

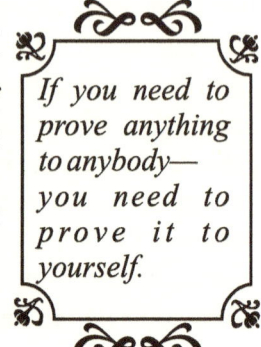

If you need to prove anything to anybody— you need to prove it to yourself.

I was teaching a lesson on how God wanted people to own their own business and real estate. After she heard the lecture she went full steam ahead in starting a business of some sort. In actuality, she became a health trainer. She lost weight, got in shape, and went out into the wilderness looking for clients. My wife and I signed up because we saw that she was so dedicated to her cause. This experience perhaps served as the paramount for her to see that she could truly be dedicated to achieving her objectives.

Debra and I asked her to help us with the proper diet and exercise plan and she dedicated herself to us like we were a million dollar project. She prepared our meals three days a week and worked our tails off with exercise four days a week. Little did she know that I was measuring her success by gauging if she would keep her routine up without wavering, she would develop qualities that she only dreamed of. I knew that if she could maintain a high commitment level to herself and to my wife and I, she would have developed a greater degree of discipline and character that would enable her to go further and higher than she ever expected.

Her drive was relentless and her desire was a burning passion. She connected to fitness like heat to fire and touched so many lives during her new discovered venture. Unfortunately, this was not her lifelong calling. This area of business served as a launching pad, not a sleeping pad. It was from this point that she would hear me share on the principles of success and finding your niche. Every person has a gift or talent that they may not be fully aware of. God hid a treasure in every person. Most people look to find it in all the wrong places. Who would think to discover a wonderful treasure inside a container full of hurt and disappointment?

This young woman was stirred up and ready for action. If I had 50 people with the same attitude that she has when it comes to going for the gusto, I would be able to do more in such a small amount of time. She and her potential partner decided to come together to start a business and came to me for advice. You can read about their business in my book, *"Building Wealth from the Ground Up."* My advice was simple and theirs were excuses. Once I challenged their every objection, they were able to move ahead and make their business a success.

Just to think that this woman had all the odds working against her. Coming from a life of obscurity and an abusive relationship, she surely is a model of success. She will never work for another person again. In order to be your own boss, you must have developed character and discipline because without these qualities, a person will have to depend on others to make decisions for them. She stands out of all the women in business and those that are educated. One day, she will stand before great people and many doors will be opened to her. And if the doors are closed, she has the keys that will thrust her through any opportunity she desires to pursue.

Chapter 3

His Money is Your Business

Chapter 3

His Money is Your Business

This chapter is written to wives that don't care to know about the family's finances. I sold insurance for years and it never ceased to amaze me of the ignorance of many wives concerning the financial matters of their family. Many of them simply leave financial matters to their spouse and would like to have nothing to do with them.

Any married woman today is likely to fall into one of these three categories, Death, Divorce or Disability. Take note of these astounding statistics...

- Nearly 80% of married women will become widows and remain widows for an average of 15 years.
- Over one-half of all marriages will end in divorce.
- If the husband is 40 or younger he is three times more likely to be disabled than to die.
- Most women choose to be naïve about her husband's money management

skills...as long as she has money to spend and to run the operations of the home.

For the many years that I sold life and health insurance and investments, there is one thing that stands out in at least 80% of the homes where the husband was the manager of the family finances, and that was that there were a high percentage of women who were completely unaware of the condition of their family's finances. At least 40% of the young men from ages 18 through 30 still had their mothers name as the beneficiary on their life insurance policy, although they were married with children. Let's face it...death usually comes at an inopportune time. Family members are employed to play hide and go-seek in order to find the necessary documents needed to complete the burial arrangements and to bring closure and financial liberty for the widow and children left behind. This is never a pleasant experience when an insurance man delivers a check for the widow but it is quite rewarding when in most cases the check is more than sufficient to take care of the family for many years.

I believe every family ought to sit down and go over all the necessary important papers in case of a sudden death. I know... no one expects it to happen to them, but the truth of the matter is that we cannot control every circumstance. Nevertheless, we can properly prepare for situations just like these. I recommend every wife to follow through with eight things:

1. Force yourself to become acquainted and comfortable discussing family money matters with your spouse.
2. Leave nothing up to chance with your financial future.
3. Sit down with your spouse and ask questions about life policies, investments, savings and checking accounts, college funds and most of all, wills.
4. If you have teen-aged children, inform them on where your important family documents can be located.
5. Don't be afraid to discuss death. Your children will appreciate that you love them enough to leave an inheritance for them.
6. Make provisions for the surviving spouse.
7. Rent a safety deposit box for safekeeping of all your important documents.
8. Don't delay, hesitate, or procrastinate. Start the process today! Don't be concerned with finishing everything in one day…just start!

If a woman engages herself in these eight things, she will develop a vigilance that will keep her on her toes and her future secured. Life is more than just trying to make a marriage, family and business work. Life is also being able to continue to live comfortably after these things cease to work. There is nothing wrong with preparation, but everything is wrong with procrastination.

> *There is nothing wrong with preparation, but everything is wrong with procrastination.*

I love my Mama, my wife and my daughters, and I just want life to be better for the women that have touched my life down through my years of being on this planet.

Developing A Champion Spirit – in just 10 minutes

Chapter 4

Understanding the Principle of Money

Chapter 4

Understanding the Principle of Money

This chapter is to help women understand the principle of money and how it works. Men and women are generally different when it comes to money issues. Statistically, men are better at math than women, but this is no indication that men are generally smarter. The basic nature of the man is that of a predator and the basic nature of the woman is that of a prey. Because of the difference in nature, men are more aggressive when it comes to making money. Men dominate the stock market and the corporate world, going after money like it is the grand prize of life. Women on the other hand, have a gentler approach toward money that may not necessarily be conducive to generating a lot of it. So, my aim is not for women to become obsessive with obtaining wealth, but to rather see the other side of how to generate the wealth for your family's future. When all has been said and done, you will not be penalized by God for being poor. Your ignorance would simply block you from enjoying the many things in life that wealth gives you the opportunity of enjoying.

Jesus taught us that a man's life does not consist in the abundance of his possessions. But He also taught us to be responsible stewards over the wealth that we have obtained. Money is an illusion. It causes people to think more of themselves, than who they actually are. Money creates a false sense of confidence, but it is never lasting. If you learn to handle money, money will never be able to handle you.

> **Eccl 9:14 (NIV)** There was once a small city with only a few people in it. And a powerful king came against it, surrounded it and built huge siege works against it.
> **15** Now there lived in that city a man poor but wise, and he saved the city by his wisdom. But nobody remembered that poor man.

This is a wealthy Poor Man. He is wealthy in wisdom, but poor in resources. You would think that with his wisdom, he would have been wise enough to learn the principle behind how money works. Money is to each of us whatever we want it to be. Allow me to tell you about money and its potential. Money itself is powerless and motionless. It has no legs to move, arms to reach, hands to touch, emotions to feel, mouth to speak, mind to think, ears to hear, or body to claim. Yet money has done all of the above, without any of the stated physical faculties. Money is a powerful powerless entity. It is the most tangible intangible; the most insensitive sensitivity. It can attract and repel at the same time. Money has no emotions, biases, fears, desires, principles or morals. So, how does money respond to people? Is it magical or mystic? How can people claim that money talks, but it has no mouth or tongue in order to speak.

> Example:
> Here lies $100 (cash); here is another $100 dollars (check); here lies $100 (IOU written on paper). Drum roll, please!
>
> Will the real money please stand up! Which one is the real $100 dollars?

Money has no real intrinsic power. Don't forget, money is powerless, yet powerful. If it is powerful, then where does it get its power? Men give money its power. In prison the inmates have very little money, so they create other forms of money with cigarettes and with this they trade and negotiate their way through prison. Can you believe this! Cigarettes are now established as a new form of money in prison. In fact, cigarettes have more value than money in prison. Therefore, money is what people have determined it to be.

Money can be gained and lost without ever revealing itself. Why? Money is relative. Money can be created out of thin air; plain paper; or even rocks for that matter. Money will be whatever people have determined it to be. Millions of people receive compensation for their labor and never see the actual cash. Money is electronically moved from one place to another without seeing the actual cash. People write checks based on thier bank records and use credit cards while never physically moving money. Therefore, all three forms of one hundred dollars stated above are real.

The basic understanding that one should have concerning money is that it is relative. If you understand the principle of money and how it is produced, you will one day be a wealthy person. Money is tantamount to the items traded for it. Men and women dance for it, sing for it, work for it, lie for it, cheat for it, and yes, give sex for it. Never negotiate your self-worth for money, or else you will become just as cheap as the paper the dead presidents are printed on. Remember, your talents, ideas, knowledge, and wisdom is worth trading for the dollars in someone else's pockets. People or companies cannot pay you what you're worth, but they can pay you what you ask for!

Chapter 5

The New Power Women

Chapter 5

The New Power Women

The Bible reveals a story about a woman whose husband had died and he left the family in debt to its creditors. The man was a prophet of the Lord and served in Elisha's school of prophets. The wife of the deceased went to Elisha concerning the debt he left with his creditors and how the creditors were coming to take her two sons to work for them for seven years in order to payoff her debts. Elisha saw her desperation, but he also had insight into her drive as a potential business woman.

Elisha asked her, "What do you have in your house?" His question was not unwarranted. His notion was to turn her into a business woman, so that she could get her family from under the power of her creditors. Her reply was, "All I have is a little jar of oil." It may have seemed insignificant to her, but it spoke volumes to Elisha. Businesses are usually started on a borrowed buck and a prayer. Elisha said go and borrow a lot of jars from your neighbors and don't just borrow a few. In other words, be aggressive in your borrowing tactics. When her and her sons collected all the borrowed jars, Elisha said go into your house and close the door and start pouring the oil from your small jar of oil into all the borrowed jars.

The secret to her success was to follow the instructions of her mentor. She did exactly as Elisha had said. She poured until all the jars filled and then the oil ceased. She was trying to figure out what she would do with all those jars of oil, so she went to Elisha and said, "I did what you asked me to do." Elisha said, "Go out and sell the oil, pay your debts and you and your sons live on the rest." From this one phrase in the Bible, the Lord gave me a divine revelation of generating income and getting out of debt. Sometimes, desperate situations cause for calculated measures. This woman was not only able to pay her debts, but to live comfortably for the rest of her life. One idea from a life or business coach can gross you millions.

Nearly eight million businesses in the United States are now owned and are operated by women, and this number is growing at a phenomenal rate. In fact, estimates are such that women-owned firms in the U.S. now provide jobs for 18.5 million people and generate sales of nearly 2.3 trillion annually. According to recent studies conducted by the U.S. Census Bureau and the National

Developing A Champion Spirit – in just 10 minutes

Foundation for Women Business Owners, this trend is only expected to increase. Below are several findings from these studies.

- Between 1987 and 1996, the number of women-owned firms has grown 78 percent.

- Employment by women-owned firms has increased by more than 100 percent from 1987-1992, compared to an increase of 38 percent in employment by all firms. For women-owned companies with 100 or more workers, employment has increased by 158 percent - more than double the rate for all U.S. firms of similar size. Women entrepreneurs are taking their firms into the global marketplace at the same rate as all U.S. business owners.

- The top growth industries for women-owned businesses between 1987 and 1996 were construction, wholesale trade, transportation, agribusiness and manufacturing.

- Women-owned businesses stand the test of time. Nearly all women-owned firms in business in 1991 were still in business 3 years later, compared to 2/3 of all U.S. firms.

- The largest share of women-owned businesses continues to be in the service sector. More than half (52 percent) of women-owned firms are in services 19 percent are in retail trade and 10 percent are in finance, insurance and real estate.

Employment growth in women-owned businesses exceeds the national average in nearly every region of the country and in nearly every major industry. More women than men now shop online, according to a report by the Pew Internet and American Life Project. For years men have been more likely to shop over the Internet than women, but in the 2001 holiday season 58 percent of those making online purchases were women, the report said.

Women also were more likely to enjoy the experience, with 37 percent reporting that they enjoyed shopping online "a lot" compared with 17 percent of men. Twenty-nine percent of men polled said they did not enjoy shopping online at all, compared with 15 percent of women. Users were more likely to say online shopping saved them time and money. New users, young users, African-Americans and Hispanics were among the most enthusiastic, the report said.

More than one quarter of those who bought online did so for the first time this year, the report found. While middle-income households earning between $30,000 and

Developing A Champion Spirit – in just 10 minutes

$50,000 showed gains, more affluent households still made up the majority of online shoppers. Three-quarters of U.S. Internet users did not buy holiday gifts online this year, citing fears of credit-card abuse, a lack of interest, and a desire to see the items before they purchase them. The report was based on a survey of 4,052 U.S. adults that took place between Nov. 19 and Dec. 23. It has a margin of error of plus or minus 2 percentage points.

Women are rapidly becoming a dominant force in business, automotive purchases, and business travel...and are surpassing men in the use of the Internet to manage it all. In January 2002, women surpassed men as online shoppers. ABC and CNN both reported that women comprise more than 52% of all online users, a trend expected to continue to rise to more than 75% within the next two years.

The facts are this; women purchase more than 50% of all new vehicles, 48% of all used vehicles, influence 80% of all sales, comprise 40% of all business travelers, influence 80% of all luxury and family travel, own 38% of all US businesses contributing $1.6 trillion to the national economy, and have now reached 52% of all Internet users.

Women also comprise 40% of all business travelers today, up 5000% since 1970. And, women take more all-female adventure tours than ever before in history spawning a new sub-travel industry of adventure travel and women-only tours. If you're a woman who has doubted the position of women in business or of women's power in economics, this report should motivate you to push even the more.

Moms, single mothers, singles (never been married), divorcees, and widowers, get up and stop feeling sorry for your self. You have some powerful women who have laid the foundation for you to experience success in life. I believe in your ability, do you? No excuses, stop procrastinating! The world is waiting to hear from you. Your spouse and children already know that you have it in you. Show them your true colors and rise in your brilliance. My wife and I work together and without her I would have an extra rib. (Smile)

Developing A Champion Spirit – in just 10 minutes

Chapter 6

Secrets to
Personal Success

Chapter 6

Secrets to Personal Success

Success in anything does not come by accident. Your success must be deliberate. If you achieve any amount of success by chance or happenstance, you will lose it when you encounter your first challenge. The reason why the percentage of lottery winners filing bankruptcy is so high is because they have never learned the lessons on how to handle money when they did not have much of it.

Your present capacity for where you are in life at this time may be only 6 inches in diameter (example). If you happen to win a lot of money through some state lottery, this is not an indication that your capacity has expanded.

> *You can never live beyond your knowledge level.*

Your money may increase but your capacity in character or life remains the same. Thus, as you continue to expose your new acquired wealth to purchases, your income will rapidly diminish to your actual 6 inches in diameter size of money knowledge. You can never live beyond your knowledge level. Personal success comes from increasing your knowledge base which causes your capacity to expand. How you handle money, relationships, and business is indicative of what you have been taught about these areas. Let me give you a brief synopsis on how you can improve your personal success.

First, define what personal success is to you. There is no crime in thinking that "having more money" is how you define success. A problem exists if money is the only element that will help you define success. Everyone needs money in our society, and you should not think that you are any different. Be honest with yourself. What secret motive prowls behind your desire? Would you like to show the naysayer that you did it without them or in spite of their lack of belief in your ability to succeed? If so, making more money will not only ruin you, but it will be used as a device to destroy other people. Genuinely change your motivation for wanting wealth, and convert it for the betterment of mankind and you will attract wealth from all sides.

Secondly, don't become inflexible as though you already have all the answers.

Accomplishment only occurs when an extensive time in training finally meets up with one moment of opportunity. People are turned off by know-it-alls. Usually the one who feels they can do it without anyone's help will show that they cannot do without anybody's help.

My sales mentor once demonstrated one of the most simplistic ways of obtaining referrals. Everybody wants to help others that want to be helped and no one wants to help anyone who acts as if they need none. Simply say to your client after giving them your best service, "I need your help!" Briefly mention how they've helped you to help them and that you would like to help their friends and loved ones as well. And watch those referrals start pouring out to you. NO feeling is better than knowing that you had a hand in someone else's success.

> *NO feeling is better than knowing that you had a hand in someone else's success.*

Thirdly, believe in yourself! You are your greatest asset and it's about time you start treating yourself like you are. One of the hardest thoughts to control is the one concerning you. All of what you can ever accomplish already exists within you. You are the cause to where you are and you will be the one to propel yourself to where you're going.

If you are interested in reading more about developing your personal success, I recommend another one of my great books. ***"BEYOND ORDINARY: Success is Only A Thought Away"*** is just the book for you. Invest in your life's education with the purchase of this book because this book is a real-confidence booster.

Developing A Champion Spirit – in just 10 minutes

Medallions of Honor

Chapter 2 "Women Overcoming Self-Doubt"
❦ *The power of the woman is concealed in her ability to hide her pain.*

❦ *If you need to prove anything to anybody— you need to prove it to yourself.*

Chapter 3 "His Money is Your Money"
❦ *There is nothing wrong with preparation, but everything is wrong with procrastination.*

Chapter 6 "Secrets to Personal Success"
❦ *You can never live beyond your knowledge level.*

❦ *NO feeling is better than knowing that you had a hand in someone else's success.*

Notes

About the Author

Dr. Mikel Brown is an author, businessman, and religious leader who resides in El Paso, Texas with his wife and two children. He is the President and CEO of CJC Enterprises and owner and CEO of Power Communications Network, through which he conducts seminars and special events. His much sought after style of communicating and humor has made him a favorite for business conclaves and church conventions.

The 3 Secrets of Money

You can hear "The 3 Secrets of Money" absolutely FREE. All you have to do is log on to www.buildinguwealth.com and scroll to the bottom right and click.

Testimonials

I listened to the online lecture at least three times just to gain a proper and healthy perspective of money. I'm making more money than ever before with my talents.

--Musician

Attracting more money has never been easier! The knowledge gained from this lecture caused me to take a introspection of why my income wasn't increasing. Having the knowledge about money is money in the bank.

--Teacher/Business Owner

You are welcome to log onto my website and sign up for your FREE Ezine which is full of wealth building tips and motivational writings that can give you a kick start in starting your own business or negotiating a better salary.

Go to www.BuildingUWealth.com and order the many freebies just for you.

NEW RELEASE

3 Powerful New Books from Dr. Mikel Brown

Gods Wants You Healthy, Wealthy & Full of Life

Your capacity to achieve, to have the life you want to have, to be the person you want to be will increase tenfold, because after reading this book you will then possess the keys to a better life. Knowing these special tips will make you more powerful and your life will change for the better.

$11.99

Developing a Champion Spirit - in just 10 Minutes for Women Only

The Greatest Gold-Mine Of Easy Advice For Women Ever Crammed Into One Book!!

Check out the table of Contents:
- Developing the Champion in You
- Women Overcoming Self-Doubt
- His Money is Your Business
- Understanding the Principle of Money
- The New Power Women
- Secrets to Personal Success

$9.95

Developing a Champion Spirit - in just 10 Minutes for Men Only

How to Accomplish Anything You Want in Life.

Check out the table of Contents:
- Developing the Champion in You
- Changing Men in Changing Times
- The Portrait of a Leader
- Exercising Your Power to Dominate
- Principles for Commanding Mountains and Overcoming Obstacles

$9.95

Beyond Ordinary -- Success is Only A Thought Away

The Average Person's Textbook, The Rich Man's Manual.

Your treasure is safe and secured, neatly stored away in your mind. You have a treasure that is presently producing nominal success; "Beyond Ordinary" will show you how to manufacture materially what is in you mentally and spiritually.

$11.99 If Bill Gates, Michael Jordan, Oprah Winfrey, Donald Trump, Dr. Mikel Brown, or TD Jakes can do it; you can do it, too!

..Money Matters..

This Powerful Package will unleash the Financial Harvest in your lifetime!

- **Start Building Your Personal WealthFoundation**
- **Gain Confidence To Start Living Your Dreams**
- **Building Wealth Success Budget Worksheets**
- **Learn The Ten Commandments of Money**
- **Break The Mentality of "Just Enough'**

Only $55.00

www.BuildingUWealth.com

Power Comminacaitions Newtork * 1208 Sumac Dr* El Paso, Tx 79925

www.ingramcontent.com/pod-product-compliance
Lightning Source LLC
Chambersburg PA
CBHW060341080526
44584CB00013B/871